Ancient Egypt

Stephanie Warren Drimmer

NATIONAL
GEOGRAPHIC

Washington, D.C.

For Mom, who loves golden treasures and creepy mummies with equal enthusiasm —S. W. D.

Designed by YAY! Design

Library of Congress Cataloging-in-Publication Data
Names: Drimmer, Stephanie Warren, author.
Title: Ancient Egypt / by Stephanie Warren Drimmer.
Description: Washington, DC : National Geographic Kids, [2018] | Series: National Geographic kids readers. Level 3 | Audience: 006-009. |
Identifiers: LCCN 2017038021 (print) | LCCN 2017041000 (ebook) | ISBN 9781426330445 (e-book) | ISBN 9781426330452 (e-book + audio) | ISBN 9781426330421 (pbk.) | ISBN 9781426330438 (hardcover)
Subjects: LCSH: Egypt--Civilization--To 332 B.C.--Juvenile literature.
Classification: LCC DT61 (ebook) | LCC DT61 .D73 2018 (print) | DDC 932/.01--dc23
LC record available at https://lccn.loc .gov/2017038021

The author and publisher gratefully acknowledge the expert content review of this book by Jennifer Houser Wegner, Ph.D., Associate Curator, Egyptian Section, Penn Museum, and the literacy review of this book by Mariam Jean Dreher, Professor of Reading Education, University of Maryland, College Park.

Author's Note

The cover features Tutankhamun's golden face mask and the title page shows the pyramids of Giza in Egypt. The table of contents photo is a painted wooden head of the pharaoh Tutankhamun.

Photo Credits

AL = Alamy; GI = Getty Images; NGIC = National Geographic Image Collection; SS = Shutterstock

Cover, Kenneth Garrett/NGIC; header, Fedor Selivanov/SS; vocab, Grishankov/SS; 1, Shotshop GmbH/AL; 3, DeAgostini/GI; 4, Hulton-Deutsch Collection/Corbis/Corbis via GI; 5, DEA/GI; 6, Space Frontiers/GI; 7, Eye Ubiquitous/UIG via GI; 8–9, Robert W. Nicholson/NGIC; 9, Robert Harding/AL; 10, Torleif Svensson/GI; 11, De Agostini/G. Sioen/GI; 12 (UP), De Agostini/A. Jemolo/GI; 12 (LO), Ramin Talaie/Corbis via GI; 13, Anton_Ivanov/SS; 14–15, Daily Travel Photos/AL; 16, C.F. Payne/NGIC; 17, Mark Lehner; 18, DEA/GI; 19, Petr Bonek/AL; 20–21, Prisma Archivo/AL; 22, J.D. Dallet/age fotostock/AL; 23, Stefano Bianchetti/Corbis via GI; 24, Kenneth Garrett/NGIC; 25, CM Dixon/Print Collector/GI; 26 (UP), DeAgostini/GI; 26 (CTR), Peter Horree/AL; 26 (LO), jsp/SS; 27 (UP), Jules Gervais Courtellemont/NGIC; 27 (CTR), Brian Kinney/SS; 27 (LO), CM Dixon/Print Collector/GI; 28, Ann Ronan Pictures/Print Collector/GI;29 (UP), Ann Ronan Pictures/Print Collector/GI; 29 (LO), DeAgostini/GI;30, DeAgostini/GI; 31 (UP), SSPL/GI; 31 (LO LE), SSPL/GI;31 (LO RT), Werner Forman/Universal Images/GI; 32, Christophel Fine Art/UIG via GI; 33, David Degner/GI; 34, DEA/G. Dagli Orti/De Agostini/GI; 35 (UP), S. Vannini/De Agostini/GI; 35 (CTR), Heritage Image Partnership Ltd/AL; 35 (LO), Werner Forman/Universal Images Group/GI; 36, William West/AFP/GI; 37, Werner Forman/Universal Images Group/GI; 38, Universal History Archive/UIG via GI; 39 (INSET), Bettmann/GI; 39, DEA/G. Dagli Orti/De Agostini/GI; 40 (INSET), Mark Thiessen/NGIC; 40, courtesy DigitalGlobe and Sarah Parcak; 42–43, Art Kowalsky/AL; 42 (INSET), DeAgostini/GI; 44 (UP), Apic/GI; 44 (CTR), bumihills/SS; 44 (LO), Khaled Desouki/AFP/GI; 45 (UP), Dan Breckwoldt/SS; 45 (CTR LE), Universal History Archive/UIG via GI; 45 (CTR RT), DEA/G. Dagli Orti/De Agostini/GI; 45 (LO), Werner Forman/Universal Images Group/GI; 46 (UP), Hulton-Deutsch Collection/Corbis/Corbis via GI; 46 (CTR LE), DeAgostini/GI; 46 (CTR RT), Patrick Landmann/GI; 46 (LO LE), Stefano Bianchetti/Corbis via GI; 46 (LO RT), Fotografiche/SS; 47 (UP LE), J.D. Dallet/age fotostock/AL; 47 (UP RT), Ramin Talaie/Corbis via GI; 47 (CTR LE), Mark Lehner; 47 (CTR RT), Federico Rostagno/SS; 47 (LO LE), courtesy DigitalGlobe and Sarah Parcak; 47 (LO RT), photoDISC

National Geographic supports K–12 educators with ELA Common Core Resources. Visit natgeoed.org/commoncore for more information.

Printed in the United States of America
20/WOR/3

Table of Contents

Peek Into the Past

It took Howard Carter years of searching before he found Tutankhamun's tomb.

On November 26, 1922, archaeologist (AR-kee-OL-uh-jist) Howard Carter stood in front of a sealed door. It had been closed for 3,000 years. His hands shaking, Carter chipped a hole in the door and peered inside.

Q What did the little Egyptian say when he woke up from a nightmare?

A "I want my mummy!"

"Can you see anything?" asked a member of his team.

"Yes," said Carter. "Wonderful things."

Carter had found the tomb of the king Tutankhamun (TOOT-ank-HA-mun). It sparkled with treasures. The discovery gave people a glimpse of one of the greatest civilizations in history: ancient Egypt.

Tomb Talk

ARCHAEOLOGIST: A person who studies objects like old tools, pottery, and tombs to learn about human history

CIVILIZATION: The culture and way of life of a group of people

a replica of the tomb that Carter and his team found

Gift of the Nile

The Nile is one of the longest rivers in the world.

Egypt is a hot, dry desert. But the Nile River runs right through it. The Nile used to flood every year. The flood water left behind thick soil called silt. The silt was good for growing crops.

People settled along the Nile more than 7,500 years ago. To keep track of when they should plant crops, they made a calendar based on the Nile's yearly flood. It had a year of 365 days divided into 12 months. We still use this calendar today.

The banks of the Nile River are green with plants and trees. Just beyond it, the desert land is dry and sandy.

Egyptian sailboats got extra power from rowers. Long poles were used to steer the boats.

Egyptians used the Nile like a highway through their land. They built boats and steered them up and down the river. The boats carried things to trade with other countries.

Ancient Egypt grew into a powerful civilization. It was one of the most powerful in the history of the world. It lasted for nearly 3,000 years, from 3150 B.C. to 30 B.C.

Date Details

The year A.D. 1 is the first year in the calendar we use today. The time of ancient Egypt was before that. Historians decided to count the time before the year A.D. 1 by counting backward from that year. They called those years B.C. For example, King Tutankhamun was born in 1341 B.C. He became king in 1332 B.C., when he was nine years old.

A.D. calendar we use today

B.C.

A.D. 2500
A.D. 2000
A.D. 1500
A.D. 1000
A.D. 500
Year 1
500 B.C.
1000 B.C.
1500 B.C.
2000 B.C.
2500 B.C.
3000 B.C.
3500 B.C.

It's Good to Be King

a statue of the pharaoh Ramses (RAM-seez) II

The rulers of ancient Egypt were called pharaohs (FAIR-ohs). People believed the pharaoh was a god on Earth.

The pharaoh had all of the power. He or she made the laws. The pharaoh owned the land and everything in it.

Artists carved and painted pharaohs onto statues and buildings. They always made the pharaoh appear young and fit—no matter how he or she looked in real life!

This stone carving shows a pharaoh with a god.

Ramses II was one of ancient Egypt's most important pharaohs. He ruled for 65 years and built more monuments than any king before him.

Tutankhamun only ruled for 10 years. But he's famous because he was buried with more than 5,000 treasures like thrones, jewelry, a gold coffin, and a chariot.

In Tutankhamun's tomb, a throne and a chariot (CHAIR-ee-uht) were discovered.

Queen of the Nile

Most pharaohs were men—but not all. For a long time, experts didn't know the pharaoh Hatshepsut was a woman. That's because she ordered statues and paintings to show her as a man—with a beard and big muscles!

a statue of Hatshepsut

Tomb Talk

CHARIOT: A two-wheeled vehicle pulled by horses

Mighty Monuments

Some pharaohs ordered huge structures called pyramids to be built. The pyramids honored the pharaohs. One was the Great Pyramid of Khufu (KOO-foo) at Giza. It was the tallest structure in the world for more than 3,800 years. It was 481 feet tall and took 20 years to build.

the Great Sphinx of Giza

The Egyptians created the Great Sphinx (SFINKS) to guard the pyramids. This statue is as tall as the White House. Its paws are bigger than city buses.

Tomb Talk

SPHINX: A made-up creature with a lion's body and a human head. Egyptians carved sphinx statues to guard important areas.

In this painting, thousands of workers build Pharaoh Khafre's pyramid at Giza.

The workers who built the pyramids did not have machines. Experts think they cut stone from quarries into huge blocks. They dragged the blocks to boats and floated them down the Nile. Then, they hauled the blocks up ramps into place on the pyramid.

Lost City

In 1999, an ancient town near the pyramids was discovered. Long ago, this town was home to workers who built the pyramids. The area was bigger than 10 football fields!

People carefully dig up the ancient town.

Tomb Talk

QUARRIES: Areas where rocks are cut from the ground for building projects

17

Life After Death

The pyramids weren't just buildings. They were tombs. A pharaoh was buried in each of the large pyramids. Smaller pyramids nearby held the bodies of family members.

Animals in the Afterlife

Not all mummies were human. Egyptians sometimes made mummies of animals like this cat. Mummies of dogs, hawks, and even crocodiles have been discovered, too.

Tomb Talk

MUMMY: The body of a human or animal that has been dried and wrapped before burial

treasures from the tomb of Tutankhamun

Egyptians believed in a life after death. They wanted to make sure their dead relatives would have everything they might need in the afterlife. So they stocked their tombs with things like food, clothes, furniture, and jewelry.

Experts think that the first mummies were made by accident. Egyptians buried their dead in the desert. The hot, dry sand killed bacteria that cause the body to break down. So instead of rotting, the bodies dried out.

This Egyptian mummy now lies in the National Archaeological Museum in Madrid, Spain.

Not everyone was mummified. The process was so expensive that only the wealthy could afford it.

The Egyptians believed that if a person's body was preserved, his or her soul would live forever. They studied these natural mummies. They learned how to make bodies last for centuries. This process is called mummification (MUM-uh-fuh-KAY-shun).

Tomb Talk

PRESERVED: Protected from breaking down or rotting

Making a Mummy

To make a mummy, ancient Egyptians would insert a hook into the dead person's nose, pull out the brain, and throw it away.

Then they removed the liver, stomach, intestines, and lungs. They sealed them in canopic (can–OH–pic) jars. The heart was left in place.

The lids of canopic jars were often decorated with heads.

Tomb Talk

CANOPIC JARS: Special containers ancient Egyptians used to store the organs of the dead

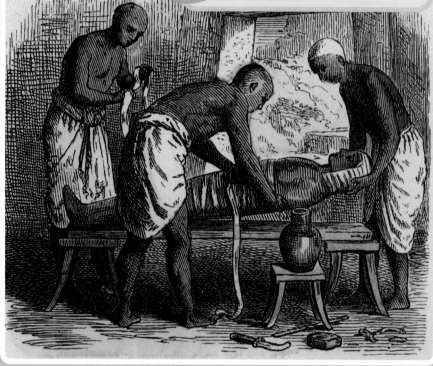

Egyptians didn't think the brain was important. They thought the heart was the source of wisdom.

Next they would pack the body with natron, a type of salt, to soak up moisture. The body was left for 40 days.

Then the natron was removed from the dried body, and the body was filled with rags to shape it. Finally, the body was wrapped in layers of linen.

In this mural from King Tutankhamun's tomb, the god Osiris (left) guides the pharaoh into the next world.

After a person died, the Egyptians believed that he or she would travel to the next world and appear before the god Osiris (oh-SY-riss). He was the judge of the dead.

The person's heart would then be weighed on a golden scale. It was weighed against a feather, called the feather of truth. If the heart weighed less than the feather, the person could live on forever in paradise.

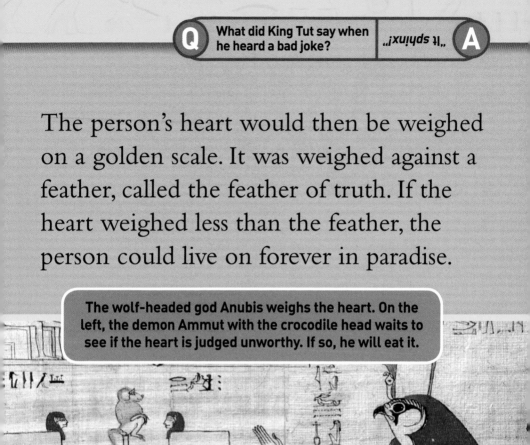

The wolf-headed god Anubis weighs the heart. On the left, the demon Ammut with the crocodile head waits to see if the heart is judged unworthy. If so, he will eat it.

6 FUN FACTS
About Ancient Egypt

1 The Egyptians thought many animals were connected with the gods, from cats, to cobras, to crocodiles.

Many ancient Egyptians shaved their heads. They did this to keep lice away and stay cool in the heat. They often wore wigs to cover their bald heads.

2

3 The Egyptians grew a lot of grain. Bread and porridge were the main meals of most people.

4

Many mummies wore masks made to look like the faces of the dead. That way the dead person's spirit could find its body again.

Of the seven big, important structures from history called the "wonders of the ancient world," the Great Pyramid is the only one still standing.

5

6

The Egyptians invented makeup. Both men and women wore it. They believed that wearing makeup gave them the protection of the gods.

Life in Ancient Egypt

Gods and goddesses were important in the everyday lives of ancient Egyptians. The Egyptians believed in more than 2,000 of them! They had a god for everything, from daily chores to a safe journey to the afterlife. Each one needed to be worshipped.

Horus was the god of the sky.

This piece of jewelry shows the falcon-headed god, Horus. In each claw, he holds an ankh, the symbol of life.

The god Thoth had the head of an ibis, a type of bird that once lived in Egypt.

Thoth (THOHTH) was the god of writing and science.

Bes (BESS) protected Egyptian families from snakes and scorpions.

The Egyptians thought the god Bes (above) also scared away demons.

Ancient Egyptians thought illness happened when the gods got angry. Doctors used spells to drive away demons. But they had medicine, too. Some didn't work, like an eye cream that included bat blood. But other medicines did. Many medicines included honey, a natural germ-killer.

This painting of a doctor treating a patient's eye is more than 3,000 years old.

Learning From Mummies

From making mummies, the Egyptians learned a lot about how the body worked. Egyptian doctors could stitch wounds, heal broken bones, and perform minor surgeries using blades.

The first known female doctor was an ancient Egyptian named Peseshet. She practiced medicine when the great pyramids were built, around 2500 B.C.

The temple of Hatshepsut was designed so that the rising winter sun would shine on a statue inside.

The Egyptians weren't just ahead of their time in medicine. They also knew a lot about math. They had to: Their tombs and temples would have toppled without it. They invented a number system based on zeros and ones that is still used to program today's computers.

They also studied the movement of the sun, moon, and stars. The Great Pyramid's four sides exactly face north, south, east, and west. Many Egyptian temples are aligned along the path of the rising sun.

a boat made of painted wood

Egyptian craftspeople made beautiful
paintings, sculptures, jewelry, and furniture.
They filled the tombs of loved ones
with these treasures. They believed
their masterpieces would come to life
once the person reached the afterlife.

Art gives us clues about what life was like
in ancient Egypt. It shows how people
dressed. It also shows what kinds of jobs
they had and what they did for fun.

a statue from the Temple of Karnak

a decorated chest

a popular Egyptian board game called senet

weird but true!

The ancient Egyptians loved board games. Some pharaohs were even buried with their favorite games.

Buried Treasure

Egyptologists (ee–jip–TAH–luh–jists) study art and ancient objects to learn what Egypt was like long ago. They carefully dig up ancient cities and peer inside tombs. They also use modern tools like 3-D scanning. They can find out what's underneath a mummy's wrappings without even taking it out of the coffin!

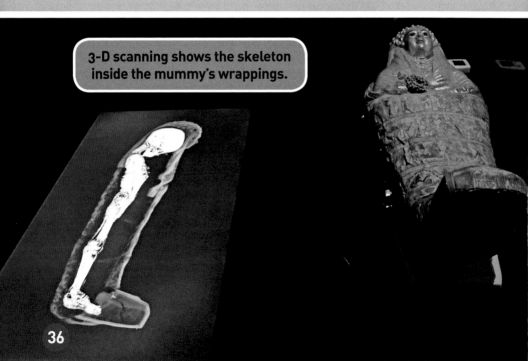

3-D scanning shows the skeleton inside the mummy's wrappings.

Tomb Raiders

Not everyone has treated mummies with such care. Ancient grave robbers broke into tombs. They unwrapped bodies to steal gold and jewels. This happened even though builders made the pyramids with tunnels and empty rooms. They did this to try to trick looters.

Ancient Egyptian police officers used trained dogs—and even monkeys! This carving shows an officer and his trained baboon arresting a thief.

Tomb Talk

EGYPTOLOGIST: Someone who studies ancient Egyptian history, language, literature, religion, architecture, or art

One of the most exciting finds from ancient Egypt happened in 1779. A French soldier discovered a stone covered with ancient writing. It was named the Rosetta Stone. The writing had the same text in three different scripts, or alphabets. One of the scripts was Egyptian hieroglyphs. This language of symbols had been a mystery for 2,000 years. Experts used the other two scripts to decode the hieroglyphs.

the Rosetta Stone

Kamal El Mallakh

Pharaoh Khufu's boat was discovered by Kamal El Mallakh in 1954.

Another big discovery came in 1954. An Egyptian Egyptologist dug up a 144-foot-long ship. It had been buried with the Pharaoh Khufu. It was built to carry the king down the Nile in the afterlife.

Ask an Egyptologist

Sarah Parcak used this satellite image to find the ancient Egyptian city of Tanis.

Sarah Parcak

Sarah Parcak uses satellite images to find lost ancient sites, like pyramids hidden beneath sand and forests.

Q: Why did you become an Egyptologist?
A: I've been in love with Egypt since I was little.

Q: Describe your job in three words.

A: Adventure. Mystery. Beauty.

Q: What's your favorite thing about excavating ancient sites?

A: The team spirit on a dig. It's like family.

Q: If you were an ancient Egyptian, what job would you want?

A: Pharaoh, of course!

Q: What advice do you have for kids who want to be Egyptologists?

A: Study hard in school and read a lot.

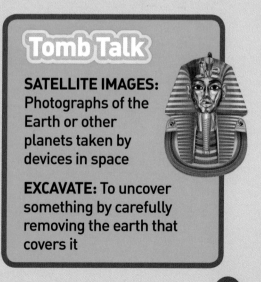

Tomb Talk

SATELLITE IMAGES: Photographs of the Earth or other planets taken by devices in space

EXCAVATE: To uncover something by carefully removing the earth that covers it

Egypt's desert sands still hold many secrets. Whose face is carved on the Sphinx? Where is the famous Queen Nefertiti buried? Egyptologists are looking for answers to these questions—and many more.

This statue is of Queen Nefertiti. She ruled alongside her husband in the mid-1300s B.C.

Does reading about pharaohs, pyramids, and mummies make you want to be an Egyptologist? Maybe someday you'll be the one to solve these mysteries!

QUIZ WHIZ

How much do you know about ancient Egypt? After reading this book, probably a lot! Take this quiz and find out.

Answers are at the bottom of page 45.

1

What did Howard Carter discover in 1922?

A. the Great Pyramid
B. the Sphinx
C. the tomb of the pharaoh Tutankhamun
D. the Rosetta Stone

2

What river flows through Egypt?

A. the Amazon
B. the Nile
C. the Mississippi
D. the Khufu

3

Who was Hatshepsut?

A. a female pharaoh
B. an Egyptian doctor
C. an archaeologist
D. a male pharaoh

4

The pyramids were _____.

A. temples
B. sculptures
C. tombs
D. grocery stores

5

What did ancient Egyptians invent?

A. the calendar
B. some rules of math
C. makeup
D. all of the above

6

What discovery helped Egyptologists decode hieroglyphs?

A. the Sphinx
B. King Tut's tomb
C. the Rosetta Stone
D. the Temple of Khafre

7

Egyptian doctors could _____.

A. stitch wounds
B. heal broken bones
C. perform minor surgery
D. all of the above

Glossary

ARCHAEOLOGIST: A person who studies objects like old tools, pottery, and tombs to learn about human history

CIVILIZATION: The culture and way of life of a group of people

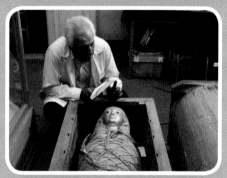

EGYPTOLOGIST: A person who studies ancient Egyptian history, language, literature, religion, architecture, or art

PRESERVED: Protected from breaking down or rotting

QUARRIES: Areas where rocks are cut from the ground for building projects

CANOPIC JARS: Special containers ancient Egyptians used to store the organs of the dead

CHARIOT: A two-wheeled vehicle pulled by horses

EXCAVATE: To uncover something by carefully removing the earth that covers it

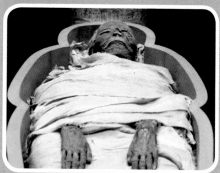

MUMMY: The body of a human or animal that has been dried and wrapped before burial

SATELLITE IMAGES: Photographs of the Earth or other planets taken by devices in space

SPHINX: A made-up creature with a lion's body and a human head. Egyptians carved sphinx statues to guard important areas.

Index